D1055231

The Cook's Own Book

The Cook's Own Book

CROWN PUBLISHERS, INC.
NEW YORK

Produced by Hearn Stephenson Publishing Ltd., London
Designed by Alan Hamp
Typesetting by Modern Word Processing Ltd.
Printed in Great Britain by
Camelot Press Ltd.
Jacket printing by Creative Print and Design

Copyright © 1982 by Hearn Stephenson Publishing Limited

All rights reserved. No part of this book may be
reproduced or transmitted in any form or by
any means, electronic or mechanical, including
photocopying, recording, or by any information
storage or retrieval system, without permission
in writing from the publisher.

First American Edition published by
Crown Publishers, Inc.
One Park Avenue, New York, New York 10016
and simultaneously in Canada by
General Publishing Company Limited.

Originally published in Great Britain by
William Collins Sons & Co. Ltd.

Manufactured in Great Britain

ISBN 0-517-54845-3

10 9 8 7 6 5 4 3 2 1

Contents

How To Use This Book

The Cook's Own Book is for you, its owner, to write. In it you can collect recipes clipped from magazines or written down by friends. You can also preserve in one place, indexed in the way you choose, kitchen hints that seem to you particularly valuable. You can also use it to keep a record of your own entertaining, and of the likes and dislikes of regular guests. It can also become the best menu planner you ever had.

On the next two pages you will find conversion tables for cooking weights and measures. Using these, you will be able to cook from any standard English-language cookbook. On pages 9 and 10 there are a number of useful care and maintenance hints to which you can add your own. Thereafter, it is almost all yours. In the *Notes* section you can add whatever you like – more hints (we have started you off with some), cookery lore (we have provided some amusing examples), lots of recipes (*The Cook's Own Book* has been specially bound to allow you to paste in material without breaking the spine) and any other snippets of information you want to keep handy in the kitchen.

Then at the back of the book you can record recipes for drinks – punches, cups, cocktails. You can keep a note of who came to dinner, with whom, what you served them and when. Use pages 175–6 to keep a note of regular guests' likes and dislikes, and of their diets too.

The last three pages are for you to write your own index. List here your trusted appetizers, main courses and desserts, the recipes for which will be in the main body of the book, so that you can plan meals in full confidence of their success and without resort to the indexes of half the recipe books in your kitchen.

The Cook's Own Book has been planned with the advice of dozens of enthusiastic and experienced cooks to help thousands more. Yours is the opportunity to make it the most useful cookbook you will ever own. The more information you add to it that you personally value, the less you will need any other cookbook in your day-by-day cooking.

Weights and Measures –
International Conversions

Weights

Approximate equivalents,
translating into
the metric system:

1oz	=	25g	(Australia: 30g)
4oz	=	100g	(Australia: 110g)
8oz	=	225g	
12oz	=	350g	
1lb	=	450g	
1½lb	=	700g	
2lb	=	900g	

Or, translating *from*
the metric system:

25g = 1oz
  (Australia: 30g = 1oz)
100g = 4oz
  (Australia: 110g = 4oz)
250g = 9oz
500g = 1lb 1oz
  (Australia: 500g = 1lb 2oz)
750g = 1lb 10oz
1kg = 2lb 3oz
  (Australia: 1kg = 2lb 4oz)

Metric Liquid Measuring System

10 milliliters (ml)	=	1 centiliter (cl)	$(= \frac{2}{5}$ fl oz)
10cl (100ml)	=	1 deciliter (dl)	$(= 3\frac{1}{2}$ fl oz)
10dl (1,000ml)	=	1 liter (l)	$(= 35$ fl oz)

Liquid Measuring Equivalents

	USA	UK	Australia/ New Zealand	Canada	Metric
1 pint	16fl oz	20fl oz	20fl oz	20fl oz	600ml
$\frac{1}{2}$ pint	8fl oz	10fl oz	10fl oz	10fl oz	300ml
$\frac{1}{4}$ pint (1 gill)	4fl oz	5fl oz	5fl oz	5fl oz	150ml

Cup Measures

(all cups = $\frac{1}{2}$ pint, local measure)

for liquids

	USA	UK	Australia/ New Zealand	Canada
1 cup =	8fl oz (225ml)	10fl oz (300ml)	8fl oz (225ml)	8fl oz (225ml)

for solids

Use the right cup measure (8 or 10fl oz) and you can work any recipe.

Spoon Measures

	USA	UK	Australia	New Zealand	Canada
1 tablespoon	$\frac{1}{2}$fl oz (15ml)	$\frac{1}{2}$fl oz (15ml)	$\frac{1}{2}$fl oz (20ml)	$\frac{1}{2}$fl oz (15ml)	$\frac{1}{2}$fl oz (15ml)
1 dessertspoon	not used	$\frac{2}{5}$fl oz (10ml)	$\frac{1}{4}$fl oz (10ml)	$\frac{1}{4}$fl oz (7ml)	not used
1 teaspoon	$\frac{1}{6}$fl oz (5ml)	$\frac{1}{5}$fl oz (6ml)	$\frac{1}{8}$fl oz (5ml)	$\frac{1}{6}$fl oz (5ml)	$\frac{1}{6}$fl oz (5ml)

The Care of Equipment

POTS AND PANS

Aluminum: If aluminum pots are badly stained boil in them either apples or a solution of a teaspoon of cream of tartar to a pint of water.

Copper: Clean tarnished copper with half a lemon dipped in vinegar and salt; when the tarnish has gone rinse in clean water and dry.

Stainless steel: Rainbow-type stains cannot be removed. Brown stains that will not come off with a mild abrasive can be removed by soaking a dishcloth in ammonia and laying it over the stain for half an hour. The stain should then come away with normal washing.

Cast iron: To remove spots and burned-on food, boil vinegar and salt in cast iron utensils. Wash them in soapy water, dry them and then coat them lightly with cooking oil.

OVENS

To clean an oven that is not self-cleaning: warm the oven, then switch it off. Put a large pan of boiling water in the bottom so that the steam can rise, and put a small pan of undiluted ammonia on the top shelf. Close the oven door and leave overnight. Then open the door, remove the pans and let the oven air for a while as ammonia fumes are toxic. When the fumes have gone, wash the oven with soap and water. If any stubborn stains remain, repeat the process as soon as possible.

To make an oven self-cleaning: If your oven is not of the self-cleaning type clean it thoroughly, as above, and then wipe it all over with a strong solution of baking soda in water. As it dries the soda will leave a slight deposit, but this will do no harm.

GLASS

Stained: A solution of salt in vinegar will remove most stains on glass, but if you cannot reach the stain (as in the bottom of a decanter), soak the stained parts overnight in false teeth cleaner.

Broken: A hand-sized piece of soft bread is better for picking small pieces of broken glass off the floor than paper towels, and much better than cloths which then have to be washed out.

Brilliant: To make glass as brilliant as possible, rinse drinking glasses in clean water to which a little vinegar has been added. Wood alcohol has a similar effect on kitchen windows and lights, retarding the build-up of airborne grease as well.

Storage: Glass can deteriorate if stored in damp conditions – it will acquire an irreversible cloudiness. Never store glass in newspaper, as it attracts damp, but use dry tissue and plastic bags. It is always wise to dry glasses after washing them, for the same reason.

Good glass: It is unwise to put high quality or decorated glass in a dishwasher. Wash by hand, one at a time, either in a plastic bowl or in a sink with a cloth spread over the bottom to soften the surface. Rinse and then drain them either on a plastic drainer or on another cloth spread on the draining board and dry them thoroughly.

SILVER

Cleaning: Ordinary cleaning of silver should be with soap and water, never with an abrasive of any kind as the surface of silver is too soft. Silver should always be dried immediately after washing and should be polished with a soft cloth only. Tarnish can be removed in two ways: either by using the best quality silver cleaner, or by immersing the silver in warm skim milk for 10 minutes, removing it and leaving it to dry, and then polishing it with a soft cloth.

Storage: Silver needs to be kept bone dry or it will tarnish. If it is to be put away for some time, wrap bone dry silver in acid-free tissue paper and then seal it in a plastic bag. Store knives, forks and spoons in regular use between layers of soft cloth in a dry place.

Notes A–Z

"ANIMALS feed themselves; men eat; but only wise men know the art of eating."
Brillat-Savarin, 1825

*

ALLSPICE: A spice in its own right, not a mixture of spices. Also known as Jamaica Pepper, it can serve as a substitute for both cloves and black pepper in cases of necessity.

*

ASPARAGUS, canned: Open cans at the bottom to minimize damage to the tips.

*

AVOCADOS: To ripen, tie avocados in a paper bag and put the bag in a warm (but not hot) place. Squeezing avocados to test their ripeness can leave bruises; a better test is to push a toothpick into the stem end: if it goes in easily, the pear is ripe.

*

APPLES, baked: Baked apples peel very easily if before cooking you slit the skin horizontally around the middle. The upper half of the skin lifts off when cooked, leaving the apple contained in the lower half.

BACON, curling: Bacon curls less when fried if it has been left in cold water for a minute or two first.

*

BREAD: "Without wishing in the slightest degree to disparage the skill and labour of breadmakers by trade, truth compels us to assert our conviction of the superior wholesomeness of bread made in our own homes."
Eliza Acton, 1855

*

BEANS, string: To revitalize tired string beans, add a pinch of sugar to the water in which they are boiled.

*

BREAD, stale: To refresh a stale loaf, run cold water over it for a few seconds, shake off any excess water and put the loaf in a moderate oven for about 10 minutes.

*

BOILING meat: If you wish to retain the goodness, add the meat to already boiling water. The heat will quickly seal the outside. If you wish to extract the goodness, as for soup, add the meat to cold water. As you bring it to the boil the juices are extracted.

*

BAY: Bay leaves complement cabbage.

B

CARROTS: ". . . the carrot serveth for love matters; and Orpheus, as Pliny writeth, said that the use hereof winneth love."
John Gerarde, 1597

*

CHERRIES: Many cherries taste bland when cooked, but retain their cherry taste much better with a very small addition of almond extract.

*

CAKES, decorating: The quickest way to decorate a cake is to put a paper doily over the top and dust with fine sugar. The larger the holes in the pattern of the doily, the more effective the decoration left behind.

*

"COFFEE is a much stronger stimulant than is commonly believed. A strong man can live a long time and still drink two bottles of wine a day, but he could not tolerate a similar quantity of coffee for so long; he would become an idiot, or die of consumption."
Brillat-Savarin, 1825

*

CUCUMBER: Some people find cucumber indigestible; it is less so if the skin is left on.

*

CABBAGE smells: To reduce the smell of boiling cabbage add lemon juice to the water.

C

C

DUCK, roasting: Roast duck can be very fatty, but if you heat the bird dry over a high heat first you can melt off much of the fat. Be careful not to let the duck burn. If a duck smells gamey before roasting and you want to reduce the gaminess, rub it with ground ginger.

*

DOUGH: "The Dough of White Bread must be thoroughly wrought, and the manner of moulding must be first with strong kneading, then with rouling to and fro, and last of all with wheeling or turning it round about, that it may sit the closer; afterwards cut it slightly in the midst round about and give it a slit or two through from the top to the bottom with a small knife, to give a vent every way to the inward moisture whilst it is in baking."
Thomas Muffet, *c.* 1595

*

DATES, chopping: Dip the knife in cold water and the dates will not stick.

*

"A dinner without cheese is like a beautiful woman who has only one eye."
Brillat-Savarin, 1825

*

DAUBE: To cook *en daube* is effectively the same as braising.

*

DRAINING vegetables: Certain vegetables once cooked never drain really dry - spinach, for example. Serve them in a bowl in which you have placed an inverted saucer and they will continue draining.

EGGS, separating: A more reliable method of separating eggs than tipping from one half shell to the other and back again is to break the egg into the palm of your hand and let the white run through your fingers.

*

EGGS, hard-boiled: If hard-boiled eggs are to be sliced, the yolk needs to be central. To ensure this happens, stir the eggs gently with a wooden spoon for their first three minutes of cooking.

*

EGGS, cracking: To avoid eggs cracking as they boil make a pin hole in the shell first.

*

EGGS, shelling: Cool hard-boiled eggs in cold running water for a minute or two, crack them and then run water between the shell and the white. Both shell and inner skin then come away easily.

*

EGGS, freshness of: Fresh eggs will sink in a bowl of cold water; stale eggs will rise.

*

EGGS, stuck to cartons: Wet the carton; the eggs will then come away without breaking.

FISH: "The land doth will, the sea doth wish, spare
sometime flesh and feede of fish."
Thomas Tusser, *c.* 1575

*

FAT, on stews: The quickest way of removing the fat that
floats to the top of stews when then are cooked is to wrap ice
cubes in paper towels and draw them over the surface of the
stew. The ice cubes chill the fat so that it begins to solidify
and stick to the paper.

*

FOIL: The point of roasting in aluminum foil is to stop meat
drying out by evaporation of its juices. The same result is
achieved by using an old-fashioned roasting pan with a lid.
If you do use foil there is no need to open it up to brown the
meat; it will brown itself inside the foil and will be more
succulent too. The shiny side of the foil should be on the
inside, next to the meat.

*

FRYING, in butter: When a recipe calls for frying in butter
you can use half butter and half oil without a significant
change in the taste of the food. The oil stops the butter
burning.

*

FISH, scaling: Fish scale more easily if rubbed with vinegar
first.

F

GRAVY, to darken: Add black coffee; it does not affect the taste.

*

GARLIC, bitterness of: To remove any trace of bitterness, bring peeled garlic cloves to the boil three times, each time in fresh water. Parsley is a good antidote if you have used too much garlic in a stew or soup: simmer a sprig or small bunch in the liquor for 10 minutes and it will reduce the strength of the garlic.

*

THE Selkirk Grace:
"Some hae meat, and cannae eat,
And some wad eat that want it,
But we hae meat and we can eat,
And sae the Lord be thankit."
Robert Burns, 1759–96

*

GLAZING pies: If a pie needs to cook a fairly long time brush it with milk before cooking and then brush with beaten egg yolk 15 minutes or so before the end. The glaze will then be a rich golden-brown without burning.

*

"GASTRONOMY is the intelligent knowledge of whatever concerns man's nourishment."
Brillat-Savarin, 1825

*

GIN: Not much used in the kitchen, but it gives a gentle juniper aroma to dishes flambéed with it.

HERBS, freezing: Sprigs of fresh herbs keep their natural taste better if dipped in olive oil before freezing.

*

HAM, ancient Roman: The 1st century A.D. recipe of Apicius: wrap a ham in a paste of oil and flour, having first made slits in the flesh into which you put honey. Enclose a generous quantity of dried figs and several bay leaves. Bake and serve as it comes from the oven.

*

HERBES, Fines: The true French mixture for *fines herbes* is equal quantities of finely chopped parsley, chives, chervil and tarragon.

*

HAMBURGERS, in quantity: To make a large number of hamburgers at once, line a baking pan with foil, add a layer of hamburgers, another sheet of foil, another layer of hamburgers and so on, up to four levels, and then bake.

*

HAM, boiled: To keep boiled ham moist and succulent, let it cool in the water in which it has been cooked.

H

ICE cubes, clear: If you dislike cloudy ice cubes, in future use cooled boiled water in the trays.

*

ICE trays, sticking: Ice trays will not stick to the bottom of the freezer if you put waxed paper under them.

*

JUICE, frozen: To mix frozen juice quickly, put it in the blender with the recommended amount of water and mix it in a few seconds.

*

JAM, crystallized: Reheat jam that has crystallized very gently, stirring occasionally, until the sugar crystals have melted. The jam will probably crystallize again, so it is best to eat it fairly soon. Crystallized honey can be treated in the same way.

*

"Stir with knife, stir in strife."
(old saying)

LEMONS, squeezing: If you are squeezing a whole lemon, try and have it at room temperature at least. Warm lemons yield more juice. If you want only a little juice from a lemon, prick it with a fork or in several places with the point of a knife. The holes will be large enough to let some juice out, but small enough to seal themselves afterward. If you cut the lemon, the cut surfaces will quickly dry out and be wasted.

*

LIVER, tough: If you suspect that a piece of liver is going to be tough, steep it in milk or wine for an hour before cooking.

*

LEMONS, lack of: Bottled lemon juice is usually cheaper than juice squeezed from fresh lemons.

*

LEMON juice, lack of: If you have no lemons or bottled lemon juice on hand for such purposes as keeping cut fruit fresh, crushed vitamin C pills mixed with water are an effective substitute.

"MAN does not live on what he eats, but rather on what he digests."
Brillat-Savarin, 1825

*

MEAT, tenderizing: When you pound meat to tenderize it, some of the juices escape. A light sprinkling of flour over the meat first reduces this loss.

*

MINT: A very little sugar sprinkled over mint as you chop it draws out the full aroma.

*

MEAT, cooking: Do not salt meat before cooking: it prevents the juices congealing properly, the meat does not seal itself quickly and so may be tough and dry. Equally, having sealed meat, do not spear it with a fork to turn it or you will lose juices. Turn it with tongs or with a spatula.

*

MUSHROOMS: Wash them under running water; if you immerse them they can absorb a lot of water. Store them in the refrigerator in a paper bag, not plastic.

"By noone see your dinner, be readie and neate, let meate tarrie servant, not servant his meate."
Thomas Tusser, *c.* 1575

*

Nuts, a substitute for: In cakes and biscuits bran gives a nutty taste.

*

Noodles: Cook noodles with a little oil in the water; the water boils less violently and the noodles do not stick together.

*

"The destiny of nations depends on how they nourish themselves."
Brillat-Savarin, 1825

*

Nasturtiums: The flowers make good decoration for summer dishes and can be eaten; the leaves are an excellent addition to salads, being a little like watercress in taste, and the seed heads can be pickled to make an adequate substitute for capers.

*

Nuts, Brazil: Much easier to shell if they have been baked in a moderate oven for fifteen minutes.

OLIVE oil: Books that advise you to deep fry in olive oil were written by Italians or for the rich. Peanut oil is very nearly as good for the purpose and much cheaper.

*

ONIONS, sautéed: If it is important that onions be an overall appetizing golden brown, sprinkle a little sugar over them as they cook.

*

OVENS: "In the building of your oven for Baking, observe that you make it round, low roofed, and a little Mouth; then it will take less fire, and keep in the Heat better than a long oven and high roofed, and will bake the Bread better."
Hannah Glasse, 1747

*

OREGANO: For culinary purposes, though not for botanical, oregano is the same thing as marjoram.

*

OYSTER plant: Another name for salsify.

*

ONIONS and tears: The colder the onion the less it will make you cry; peeling under running water also helps, and so does leaving cutting the base until last.

PIES: "Graceful monuments, delicious fortresses, seductive ramparts, which as soon as they are on all sides attacked, totter, crumble, and no longer present anything but glorious and ephemeral ruins, like every work of man – all pass away whether they be temples, columns, pyramids or pies."
Alexis Soyer, 1853

*

PLASTIC wrap: Is easier to handle if kept in the refrigerator.

*

"THE proper progression of courses in a meal is from the heaviest to the lightest."
Brillat-Savarin, 1825

*

PEPPERCORNS: White peppercorns are black peppercorns with the outer skin removed; their taste is sharper.

*

POTATOES, baked: To make them bake more quickly, stab potatoes all over with a fork before cooking. Rub the skins with salt if you like them crisp.

*

POTATOES, scraping: Save effort scraping new potatoes by pouring boiling water over them and leaving them to stand for a couple of minutes. The skins then come off easily.

P, Q

ROASTING, quick: If you have to roast a piece of meat
quickly, set the oven high and put in a pan of water as well
as the meat. The steam from the water reduces the risk of
scorching the outside of the meat.

*

RED cabbage: A tablespoon of vinegar added to the cooking
water stops red cabbage from going purple.

*

"For rabbits hot, for rabbits cold,
For rabbits young, for rabbits old,
For rabbits tender, for rabbits tough,
We thank Thee Lord . . . we've had enough."
Dean Swift, 1667–1745

*

RECIPES, keeping clean: An easy way to keep recipe books
clean while you are cooking is to place a glass pie plate
upside down over the open pages. The plate can also
magnify the print, making it easier to read at a distance.

*

ROLLS, hot: To keep rolls on the table warm for a longer
time, put them in a basket lined with aluminum foil.

SALT, excess: If you have too much salt in a soup or stew, add a peeled potato and boil for a few minutes. The potato will take up a lot of salt. Remove the potato.

*

STUFFING: Save time when stuffing a chicken or turkey by stopping the cavity with a raw potato instead of sewing it closed.

*

"He that eats sage in May
Will live for aye."
(old saying)

*

SALT, in salad: Add salt to lettuce at the last possible minute; salt wilts lettuce.

*

STRAWBERRIES, to keep: Strawberries will keep for several days in a refrigerator if they are kept in a colander – they need the circulation of air. Do not hull the berries until you are ready to eat them, and wash them (if you need to) before hulling, not after – the berries can absorb a lot of water if opened.

S

S

S

"THE table is the only place where a man is never bored for the first hour."
Brillat-Savarin, 1825

*

TOMATOES, to skin: A quicker way of skinning tomatoes than leaving them in boiling water is to put them on a fork and hold them over high heat.

*

TOMATOES, to ripen: Putting unripe tomatoes in direct sunlight will soften them before it ripens them. Leave them in a warm, light place out of direct sunlight.

*

TRUSSING: Unwaxed dental floss is stronger than string and is less likely to burn.

*

TURNIP, cooking smells: The smell of boiling turnip is much reduced if a little sugar is added to the water.

*

THYME: Thyme complements mushrooms.

T

VANILLA pods, buying: The best vanilla pods are coated with a frosting of white crystals.

*

VIOLETS: Crystallized violets are familiar as cake decorations, but the fresh flowers and leaves can be eaten raw in salads too.

*

"THE Universe is nothing without the things that live in it, and everything that lives, eats."
Brillat-Savarin, 1825

*

VEAL bones: Veal bones are usually the most generous with their jelly and are accordingly the best bones to use for light stock.

*

VENISON: Good venison will have fat that is clear and creamy, not yellow and hard.

*

VEGETABLES, cleaning: Remove insects from cabbage and other closely packed vegetables by soaking the vegetables untrimmed in cold water with a generous addition of salt or vinegar.

WHIPPED cream: Cream that has to be whipped well ahead of time will hold its shape and consistency better if you add a very small amount of powdered gelatin. Cream whips most easily when the bowl and the beater are chilled, as well as the cream. If cream won't seem to whip at all, add the white of an egg and try again.

*

WALNUTS, to shell: To get the meat out in one piece, soak walnuts in salt water overnight to soften the shells.

*

YEAST dough: Yeast dough has risen as much as it is going to when a finger-dent will remain in the top of the dough. If the dent is puffed out by the dough the yeast is still working and the dough is still rising.

*

WATERMELON: A dull skin usually indicates a watermelon in better condition than a shiny skin.

*

ZUCCHINI: The Italian and American name for what the French and the English call courgettes.

Drinks

Vinum non facies bonum BIBendo. Mart. lib.5.

Entertaining
Record

ENTERTAINING RECORD

Date
_____

Guests_____
_____
Food_____
_____
Wines_____
Notes_____
_____
_____

Date
_____

Guests_____
_____
Food_____
_____
Wines_____
Notes_____
_____
_____

Date
_____

Guests_____
_____
Food_____
_____
Wines_____
Notes_____
_____
_____

Date
_____

Guests_____
_____
Food_____
_____
Wines_____
Notes_____
_____
_____

ENTERTAINING RECORD

Date
_____

*Guests*_____
_____
*Food*_____
_____
*Wines*_____
*Notes*_____
_____
_____

Date
_____

*Guests*_____
_____
*Food*_____
_____
*Wines*_____
*Notes*_____
_____
_____

Date
_____

*Guests*_____
_____
*Food*_____
_____
*Wines*_____
*Notes*_____
_____
_____

Date
_____

*Guests*_____
_____
*Food*_____
_____
*Wines*_____
*Notes*_____
_____
_____

Date

_____

*Guests*_____

_____

*Food*_____

_____

*Wines*_____

*Notes*_____

_____

_____

Date

_____

*Guests*_____

_____

*Food*_____

_____

*Wines*_____

*Notes*_____

_____

_____

Date

_____

*Guests*_____

_____

*Food*_____

_____

*Wines*_____

*Notes*_____

_____

_____

Date

_____

*Guests*_____

_____

*Food*_____

_____

*Wines*_____

*Notes*_____

_____

_____

ENTERTAINING RECORD

Date
_____

*Guests*_____
_____
*Food*_____
_____
*Wines*_____
*Notes*_____
_____
_____

Date
_____

*Guests*_____
_____
*Food*_____
_____
*Wines*_____
*Notes*_____
_____
_____

Date
_____

*Guests*_____
_____
*Food*_____
_____
*Wines*_____
*Notes*_____
_____
_____

Date
_____

*Guests*_____
_____
*Food*_____
_____
*Wines*_____
*Notes*_____
_____
_____

Date

*Guests*_____
_____
*Food*_____
_____
*Wines*_____
*Notes*_____
_____
_____

Date

*Guests*_____
_____
*Food*_____
_____
*Wines*_____
*Notes*_____
_____
_____

Date

*Guests*_____
_____
*Food*_____
_____
*Wines*_____
*Notes*_____
_____
_____

Date

*Guests*_____
_____
*Food*_____
_____
*Wines*_____
*Notes*_____
_____
_____

Date

Guests_____
_____
Food_____
_____
Wines_____
Notes_____
_____
_____

Date

Guests_____
_____
Food_____
_____
Wines_____
Notes_____
_____
_____

Date

Guests_____
_____
Food_____
_____
Wines_____
Notes_____
_____
_____

Date

Guests_____
_____
Food_____
_____
Wines_____
Notes_____
_____
_____

Date

_____

Guests_____

Food_____
_____

Wines_____
Notes_____
_____
_____

Date

_____

Guests_____
_____

Food_____
_____

Wines_____
Notes_____
_____
_____

Date

_____

Guests_____
_____

Food_____
_____

Wines_____
Notes_____
_____
_____

Date

_____

Guests_____
_____

Food_____
_____

Wines_____
Notes_____
_____
_____

Date
_____

*Guests*_____
_____
*Food*_____
_____
*Wines*_____
*Notes*_____
_____
_____
_____

Date
_____

*Guests*_____
_____
*Food*_____
_____
*Wines*_____
*Notes*_____
_____
_____
_____

Date
_____

*Guests*_____
_____
*Food*_____
_____
*Wines*_____
*Notes*_____
_____
_____
_____

Date
_____

*Guests*_____
_____
*Food*_____
_____
*Wines*_____
*Notes*_____
_____
_____
_____

ENTERTAINING RECORD

Date

_____

*Guests*_____
_____
*Food*_____
_____
*Wines*_____
*Notes*_____
_____
_____
_____

Date

_____

*Guests*_____
_____
*Food*_____
_____
*Wines*_____
*Notes*_____
_____
_____
_____

Date

_____

*Guests*_____
_____
*Food*_____
_____
*Wines*_____
*Notes*_____
_____
_____
_____

Date

_____

*Guests*_____
_____
*Food*_____
_____
*Wines*_____
*Notes*_____
_____
_____
_____

ENTERTAINING RECORD

Date
_____

*Guests*_____
_____
*Food*_____
_____
*Wines*_____
*Notes*_____
_____
_____

Date
_____

*Guests*_____
_____
*Food*_____
_____
*Wines*_____
*Notes*_____
_____
_____

Date
_____

*Guests*_____
_____
*Food*_____
_____
*Wines*_____
*Notes*_____
_____
_____

Date
_____

*Guests*_____
_____
*Food*_____
_____
*Wines*_____
*Notes*_____
_____
_____

ENTERTAINING RECORD

Date _____

Guests _____
_____

Food _____
_____

Wines _____
Notes _____
_____
_____

Date _____

Guests _____
_____

Food _____
_____

Wines _____
Notes _____
_____
_____

Date _____

Guests _____
_____

Food _____
_____

Wines _____
Notes _____
_____
_____

Date _____

Guests _____
_____

Food _____
_____

Wines _____
Notes _____
_____
_____

ENTERTAINING RECORD

Date
_____

*Guests*_____
_____
*Food*_____
_____
*Wines*_____
*Notes*_____
_____
_____

Date
_____

*Guests*_____
_____
*Food*_____
_____
*Wines*_____
*Notes*_____
_____
_____

Date
_____

*Guests*_____
_____
*Food*_____
_____
*Wines*_____
*Notes*_____
_____
_____

Date
_____

*Guests*_____
_____
*Food*_____
_____
*Wines*_____
*Notes*_____
_____
_____

Date _____

Guests _____
_____
Food _____
_____
Wines _____
Notes _____
_____
_____

Date _____

Guests _____
_____
Food _____
_____
Wines _____
Notes _____
_____
_____

Date _____

Guests _____
_____
Food _____
_____
Wines _____
Notes _____
_____
_____

Date _____

Guests _____
_____
Food _____
_____
Wines _____
Notes _____
_____
_____

Regular Guests

Likes and Dislikes

*Name*_____
*Likes*_____
_____
*Dislikes*_____
_____

*Name*_____
*Likes*_____
_____
*Dislikes*_____
_____

*Name*_____
*Likes*_____
_____
*Dislikes*_____
_____

*Name*_____
*Likes*_____
_____
*Dislikes*_____
_____

*Name*_____
*Likes*_____
_____
*Dislikes*_____
_____

*Name*_____
*Likes*_____
_____
*Dislikes*_____
_____

*Name*_____
*Likes*_____
_____
*Dislikes*_____
_____

*Name*_____
*Likes*_____
_____
*Dislikes*_____
_____

*Name*_____
*Likes*_____
_____
*Dislikes*_____
_____

*Name*_____
*Likes*_____
_____
*Dislikes*_____
_____

*Name*_____
*Likes*_____
_____
*Dislikes*_____
_____

Menu Planner

MENU.

Hors d'œ[uvres] [vari]és.

—

Sarah B[ernhardt]
Crême d[e ...]

—

Saumon, Sauce [Hollanda]ise.
Pommes Cha[teau ...]l.
Salade de Co[ncombres]
Eperlans [frits]

—

Mauviettes en Caisses f[arcies aux] Truffes.
Poulets sautés à [...]

—

Selle de Mouton, Gelé[e de Grosei]lles.
Petits Poi[s]
Pommes risso[lées]

—

Faisans.   [...]s.
Salade.

—

Compote de Prune[s]
Soufflés panachés g[lacés]
FROMAGES.   [...]RT.

Café Ro[...]
[...]e 1886.

Appetizers

Main Courses

Desserts